Mnemosyne's Hand

Mnemosyne's Hand

Charles W. Brice

9. 7. 2018

WordTech Editions

For Ben + Nancy Manthai,
Ben: Lief Erikson gave my book 5 ½
Ughs! He didn't like the political
poems because he's a conservative like
you. Still 5 ½ stars!!
  Nancy: thanks for all the good
cheer and food over the years
and for watching our dock. That's
dock.
        Love,
        Charlie

Published by WordTech Editions
P.O. Box 541106
Cincinnati, OH 45254-1106

ISBN: 9781625492760

Poetry Editor: Kevin Walzer
Business Editor: Lori Jareo

Visit us on the web at www.wordtechweb.com

For Ariel Brice, Jim Hutt, and Bill Richards

Table of Contents

I

Hot Tea

Ariel didn't speak
for almost two years. Then,
one quiet morning on Walloon Lake,
I approached the breakfast table
with a steaming pot of tea. I poured
a cup and took a sip. "Hot tea,"
Ari said, clear as a speech therapist.
This kid was no cliché.
No "mama" or "dada"
first words for him.

A couple days later he looked at us
and said, "pâté." "Pâté!"
Judy and I yelled!
"Hot tea and pâté!" we chanted,
and danced on the beach,
and held him close,
felt his warm baby breath
on our necks and thought,
hey, this kid might turn out
to be expensive!

Mnemosyne's Hand

Ten years old and transfixed, I stood
beside my baseball idol, Jim Gentile.
That year, or the next, he hit 46 homers,
made a run for the Babe's record,
only bested by the Mick with 56.
I handed Mr. Gentile the official Little League
baseball I'd brought with me all the way
from Cheyenne to LA on the promise
of seeing this game between the Orioles
and Angels. He graciously signed
my ball and I guarded that graying orb
for thirty years until Ariel, my son,
was ten years old. It was a hot Sunday
afternoon and we wanted to play ball
down at Koenig Field where there
was a backstop and canvas bases
we could run. We looked everywhere,
but couldn't find a ball, so I grabbed
the one Mr. Gentile had signed for me.
What else could I do? I can't remember
which one of us hit that ball into
the jungle of forsythia, ferns, weeds,
and brambles that lined our field,
but try as we might, and we tried hard,
we never found that ball with Jim
Gentile's name written in blue ink
between those ancient Little League
seams. I often walk past Koenig Field,
dawdle watching young parents
throw the ball with their kids,
girls now as well. The details
of the game with Ari, twenty-six
summers past, and the one Jim
Gentile played against the Angels
in 1960, have dwindled, lost

in the folds of memory. As for
that ball, the one Jim Gentile
signed, it rests in the palm
of Mnemosyne's hand, along
with the crack of a bat,
the chirp of Ari's voice,
and his smile.

Gaia's Stringy Fingers

Half way up that mountain I remembered
that I was sixty years old. The mosquitos
were as big as Russian migs with stingers
the size of nose cones. My Eddie Bauer

cotton shirt was no defense. Ari, my son,
was in his element, circling me
several times as we climbed this Big
Horn in the Wyoming wilderness.

Almost at the top, where a lake lay
near the ground we would camp,
a woman and her three kids panicked
past us down the trail in a rush.

The blood drained from her face,
her voice shook, "There's a moose
and her calf up there." Horror traced
her lips: "They kill more people

each year than any other wild animal!"
The frightened four were past us
quicker than Rocky could say "Bullwinkle."
Ari chuckled and resumed his trek

while I stood still. "I don't know
that I want to keep going," I said.
"I'm no match for an angry moose."
Ari took off his pack and patted my

arm. "Now let's think about this dad,"
his voice was gentle, "settle down,
stay calm." This role reversal
would have been funny had terror

not rampaged through my guts

like SEAL Team Six after Bin Laden.
I was not only the daddy here, but
a shrink with thirty years experience

treating anxiety—in others. "What
are you afraid of, Dad?" His face smooth,
unwrinkled by worry, head bent
to one side in the "I understand"

attitude approved by the American
Psychological Association. Before I
could respond, my inner SEAL Team
locked on their target and fired.

"I have to shit," I bellowed, took
the toilet paper, found a tree
that hid me, and assumed the ancient
position. What was it I felt

underneath me? Gaia's stringy fingers
pulling me toward my primordial
beginnings, or just tall grass? No
matter. The product of my efforts

behind the tree was momentous:
I didn't know whether to baptize it
or give it a military funeral—
a twenty-one gun salute, and a flag.

When I rejoined Ari on the trail
my fear was gone. "Let's go," I said.
Ari smiled as the two of us finished
our hike. At the top we watched

the mother moose and her calf,
in the lake of our destination, munch
on pondweed and lilies—immersed
in the peace of parent and child.

Some Indian Fella: The Big Horns, 2009

Shortly after Ari fixed our breakfast
of bacon, eggs, and potatoes and
after he filled the canteen from the stream
and treated the water with chemicals
to make it drinkable, we broke camp.
I was washing pans, plates, knives and forks,
when I heard crunching sounds,
looked up, and saw a bull moose
chomping on some dead brush
twenty feet from me. He looked
like a mountain with horns.

"Ari, what do we do?" I whisper-
yelled. "Get in the tent," Ari, our son,
whisper-yelled back, which I did
très pronto! Ari joined me, then
left to retrieve a hatchet for our defense
(like aiming a BB gun at a rhino, I thought,
but kept that to myself).

Later, in Buffalo, I asked the man
who ran the Tourist Center
what we should have done. He
tipped his hat with a calloused thumb,
adjusted his belt buckle, his chest
stretching the snaps on his white
cowboy shirt, a crooked grin
on his face. "You done

what you shoulda done," he said,
and told us about "some Indian fella"
who tried to pet a moose a few
weeks back. "That moose worked
him over pretty good," he said.
"He's still in the hospital," he clicked

air through yellowed teeth on the side
of his mouth. "And then," he said,
as if they'd fed the Indian fella
loco-weed in the hospital, "He
wanted us to shoot the moose!"

Your Name in the Lake

I wrote your name in the lake
then my name,
our son's name,
our daughter's name,
then the universe's name,
then god's name
in the lake. I swam

in our names, dove
below and felt how cool
our names were, how fresh
when our surface cracked.

I wrote your name on the brow
of your budded green profusion,
the leaf you became
stout, proud, frim—
how you trembled.
The season you had was grand
then gilded, crinkled, beldame,
you dropped
weary winds
blown undisclosed
unknown.

I breathed your name
over snail, slug, toad and turtle
their days spent
from spore to tadpole to crick scum
the abundance of life
in your name

in every writhing arroyo
of your body.

Your Mouth

Your mouth lay open
in that helpless heat,
bedsheets pulled up to your chin,
your face gray and worn out.

I thought back forty-three years:
we were to be married in August
and were grocery shopping at Safeway,
living on Race Street in Denver,

living "in sin" as they said at the time.
An elderly woman stood by the lettuce
display, her mouth agape, her faded
green greatcoat hung like a moan

from her shoulders. An old man,
clearly her husband, approached.
"Can't you shut your mouth?"
he said loud enough to humiliate her

and embarrass us. So close to our vows
we laughed nervously about this scene,
laughed about it for years. We'd never
wind up like those two rutted beings.

And now, in this dim hospital light,
I watch you gulp desperate air,
this seventeenth surgery,
these two years of pain,

a silent scream between us.
I love your open mouth.
I bend low over you and kiss
your blistered lips, blessed

by your fevered skin.
And we can still laugh about
that old man and his wife
standing by the lettuce display,

her green coat hopelessly scraping
the dirty Denver tile,
because what happened to them
never happened to us.

You're on Celestial Time Now Baby

Three nondays here

        yesternonday I compressed everything and it blew
        tononday whatever you are you are here
        tononmorrow at the last nonhour it all ends

We disappear   poof

Eternity was your invention   not mine

Only a few left here

        I had to snuff most of the Christians Muslims and Jews

They bickered loudly   argued nonday and nonnight

My eardrums already half-blown by supernovas

I snuffed Einstein too

        We had some great conversations
        but he was appalled at what his equations kept proving

        total randomness
        stuff forming out of nothing
        that sort of thing

He wouldn't shut up about it

I can't stand that kind of noise

Not only do I not play dice with the universe

I don't play with the universe

It plays with me

Clouds

All my photos are in a Cloud,
even the pictures I took of clouds—
clouds in a Cloud, a heavenly tautology.
In the Cloud are my pictures
of clouds as seen through windows.
A picture I took of Magritte's
painting of a window with clouds
on an easel next to a window

that opens onto clouds
resides now in my Cloud,
on my Windows Program.
On Walloon Lake a few years back
I saw a castle in a cloud
aglow from within by lightning,
a celestial light show.
My wife and son and I were thrilled.

One day the Maybememory Program
will open a window and I'll squeeze through.
Freed from the trammels of concrete existence,
a cloud will house whatever is
left of me and mine. I'll reside forever,
in the nether kingdom of Almostistan,
a few gigabytes down from Virtualville,
on the continent of Justabouttodisappear.

Soulium

Having doubts about why you are alive,
why things happen as they do,
why religious fanatics burn people alive,
take off heads, shoot unarmed cartoonists,
destroy ageless art works,
hang gay people because they love one another,
tell Palestinians they can't live in their own country,
decide that all Jews must die,
that women should obey men because they aren't men
and that they cannot control their own bodies,
that if you don't believe in Jesus you can't get to heaven,
that children who haven't had a chance to do anything wrong
enact God's will by dying of cancer or any other number of horrible diseases,
preach that God is all powerful and then pray to Him for help
with all the horrible things he must have caused in the first place?
Have a persistent conviction that's it's all a huge *mysterium tremendum?*

Looks like you need Soulium. Five milligrams of Soulium
taken twice a day wipes all religious and existential doubts away.
Don't take Soulium if you are allergic to excessive happiness
or mindless euphoria. Some people taking Soulium have experienced
immediate alcoholism, heroin use, or cravings for methamphetamines.
Common side effects include an inability to stop watching CNN,
extreme interest in issues and events that have no real importance
such as what email server Hilary Clinton uses
or whether the President of the United States was born in the United States.
Stop using Soulium immediately if you attain an erection that talks;
call your doctor right away if it recites anything from a Beckett play
or a Bukowski poem. Don't take Soulium if you already have a soul,
as doing so may cause a dangerous drug reaction.

Rage Rage Against the Light[1]

All nerves to serve the sun,
nerves stretched and stressed
on waves of sight and sound
found 24/7 on CNN between
commercials, shadows on the cave
wall—what to do for Vaginal Mesh
while watching the tube and eating
tapioca with appall, or Dickie
Smothers, his diseased esophagus,
no more smiles, it's precancerous.
Back to the sun: Kim Jong Il,
or his son, wants to kill us.
His quest seems evil,
keeps us edgy, in peril.

And now for this message: love,
it makes a Subaru a Subaru.
It's what you'll remember most about
Sandals Grand Antigua—falling
in love again—a perpetual grin, but not
from representative Michael Grimm
who told a reporter he'd throw him
off a balcony and break him "like a boy,"
probably a felony but not if you represent
our colony. Honesty is, of course,
the best ploy.

Now, to be rude, here's another interlude:

Wolf: What can you tell us, Anderson?
Anderson: Well the police don't have any clues.
Wolf: Ok, Anderson, let me get this straight.
You're saying they don't have any clues.
Anderson: That's right, Wolf. No clues as of yet.
Wolf: How scared should we be, Anderson?

Anderson: Really scared, Wolf.
The police don't have any clues.
Wolf: Thanks for keepin 'em honest, Anderson.
Anderson: Keepin 'em honest, Wolf.

On the tube it's goof and spoof:
stop smoking use Chantix,
who cares about the side effects.
If your dog can dream it, Purina
ProPlan can help him achieve it.
To keep your anus musical,
there's always Metamucil.
Are you guys sick of feeling fat
and tired? Try Nutrisystem,
the sex is fantastic! Supercharged
and *semper paratis*, you're always
prepared with Cialis.

The corpus of Christie jams
his constituents on a bridge
in New Jersey, makes payback
his business, and uses his hugeness
to conjure sickness, catches
the blues from the sharks
of 24 hour news, a feeding frenzy
of Rachels, Rushes, Andersons,
and Briannas who eat and eat
but never feel renewed, never
get their fill. And we, what are we
to do? Turn off the tube?
Step out of the cave?
Take another pill?
Watch and crave?

Sartre on Smoking: A Villanelle

Jean Paul lit a cig, ready for a brawl.
"I can quit any time I want to," he said,
"*mauvaise foi* is better than no *foi* at all."

"It's true, I never grew to be tall,
but not because I smoked as a kid in bed."
Jean Paul lit a cig, ready for a brawl.

"My face is covered with a pallid pall,
but I'll stop smoking well before I'm dead."
Mauvaise foi is better than no *foi* at all."

"Lead nations or get drunk alone, it's all banal.
Nothingness earned me my daily bread."
Jean Paul lit a cig, ready for a brawl.

"Sincerity sucks when you're up against a wall.
I'll refuse that fag before they put a bullet in my head.
Mauvaise foi is better than no *foi* at all."

"I wrote that Hell is other people,
pour soi present, past gone, tomorrow yet ahead."
Jean Paul lit a cig, ready for a brawl.

"To be is absurd, an existential cabal.
I prefer to puff away the dread."
Jean Paul lit a cig, ready for a brawl.
"*Mauvaise foi* is better than no *foi* at all."

The Old Manischewitz and the Lake

For Sue William Silverman

The old Manischewitz hobbled with his
fishing pole to the end of his dock,
his dock, which was attached
to his house, a clean well lit house. He

cast onto the lake, Lake Walloon,
and it was a good cast. His bones
creaked as he sat down on his dock—
his bones bleached white from the sun
even though he was still alive.

He thought about death—how she
crept toward him every day since
he got older every day and it was the way
of a man to die, eventually, when
those days added up to a large
two hearted number.

These were, he knew, existential thoughts,
even though he had no idea what
the word "existential" meant. A subtle
smile spread across his face as he
realized that, across the river of his life
and through its trees, he hadn't managed
to acquire even a farfel of wisdom.

These thoughts, the thoughts of a man
facing the edge of his dock, were
interrupted by a vicious tug on his pole
and the nothingness of his bobber which
had disappeared below the lake surface.

He gripped his pole like Robert Jordon
gripped his gun as he lay atop the pine

needle forest floor at the end of *For
Whom the Bell Tolls* and gasped because
he realized that using that scene from
For Whom the Bell Tolls, a scene that
takes place on land and in Spain,
was an insanely inappropriate metaphor
for what he now knew he had to endure.

His sun-bleached bones protesting every
move, he stood, defeated, but with grace,
and set his hook. He knew that he was in
for *une bataille épique*, for the old Manischewitz
had hooked the ferocious gefilte fish! The size
and shape of a golf ball this fish, he knew, confronted
a man with the essence of his manhood.

He fought the fish, *mano y matzo*, for nearly
minutes until, defiant but dead, the fish
lay in the man's fishnet, and now that
it was dead, the old man respected
it more than ever. But then the man
remembered that he faced the long walk
back to his house. He grimaced when
he recalled that his little son Havelock,
100 lbs. overweight and in his 30s,
had eaten, in a feeding frenzy the night
before, all the red horseradish that
the old Manischewitz always spread
on the gefilte fish when he ate it.

"There will be no red horseradish,"
the man said aloud, as much to the fish
as to anyone else. He thought of the woman
who had given birth to the 300 pound boy,
the woman who waited for him in the house.
He began his long walk in the rain
back to the house, his gefilte fish,
beautiful in death, dangling from his pole.

It was a lovely day on the lake, the rain
solely in his mind, the only place that he
could trust, that he could count on.

Rhymes With...

Mirror of myriad romances,
mother of *méconnaissance,*
tyrant of tides, lunatic lady
who locks asylum wards,

weaves her glow down dark
country roads, and when full
grows hair and claws on mythic beasts.
Huge orange orb that hovers

over harvest heath and hauls
hordes of tiny sugar heathens
through Halloween, their bulging bags
of legal extortions visible in her light.

Sphere that lent her name to an infinity
of rhymes: goon, tune, maroon, raccoon,
zoom, lagoon, lampoon, buffoon,
Cancun, baboon, monsoon, festoon,

and at whom wolves and frustrated
men, nads of blue, howl—the one
for lack of anything better to do,
the other because lack will not do,

but mostly that cool sister of sun
that burns too brightly to hide
silent moments shared by lovers
under her hoary, old-timey, halo.

Ode To A Waiting Room Chair

You are constant
in your unwavering
wooden uniformity.
You are often twins,
sometimes triplets;
an engineering miracle
of conformity. I love

your blond beauty,
the Archimedean spiral,
always the same,
on the smooth textured arms
of your processed oak,

and the soft blues
and dark pinks
of your seamless upholstery—
the calmness of that!
You are a dream
of stability. You have

no skin in the game:
you always assume
a minor, supporting, role
to my intestinal obstructions,
excruciating pain, or my pounding,
irregular heart.

You never intrude,
only enhance. You
make the scuffed
white wall an aberration,
allowing my eyes
to hide in your boring
bounty. Placed in repose

beside an institutional garbage can,
or an artificial peace plant,
its sticky plastic leaves
and black-dyed Styrofoam "dirt"—
offensive but for your
quiet grace. I love
how you pad my tushy,
not in a flamboyant
manner, but, as always
quietly, humbly, unobtrusively!
I can count on your sameness,
whether I find you at Mayo,
or the Cleveland Clinic,
or UPMC in Pittsburgh.

You remind me
of the now defunct
Latin Mass—a lost
selling point of Catholicism.
It used to be you'd hear Mass

the same anywhere
in the world. Now
the ramblings of Eucharist
are mostly incomprehensible
outside of local parishes,
but not you! Your sturdy
blandness welcomes me

in Europe, Africa,
even the Balkans!
Thank you for that!
God may have made
the tree, but our engineers
processed your glory.

You are as reassuring
as Colonel Sanders,

Starbucks, or McDonalds.
Variation, a fear we are
without! Multiplicity,
be not proud!

Ode to an Avocado

The first time I met you
I threw up. Our family was
visiting friends in Phoenix
and an evil babysitter
made me sit at the table
until I ate you. I thought
I was eating green snot.
Your smell made me think
of cousin Terry's dirty wallet
sent to us in a box
after he was killed
driving drunk in Torrington, Wyoming.
I told the baby sitter
I would vomit, but
she didn't believe me
until you, the meatloaf I ate,
and the orange juice I drank
formed a verdant pool
on our friend's dining table.

First impressions are often wrong.

Now I admire how your softness
grows in darkness, how you escape
paper bag prison rehabilitated
from hard heartedness to zaftig lover—
your beautiful black skin a womb
of exotic flavor—how your pit
teaches patience, never complains
about the toothpicks that save it
from drowning in the juice glass
on our window sill. When I cut
into you, your reluctant fruit-
ripened virtue gives way.
Your sudden breach welcomes

my probing fingers, priapic
fingers that caress and squeeze
until your seed conceives that feral fossa—
a fen for olive oil, garlic, vinegar,
sweet basil—how generous
of you to honor those flavors.
Thank you for your musky scent, your
coarse covering, your smooth interior,
your invitation to a joyous tongue.

Measuring Time

Measure time by each object left behind.
Tarfia Faizullah

For Einstein it shaped geometry,
was an identical twin of space,
cousin to matter, our favorite relative,
the most exciting square around.

Turns out, all pitches are curve balls.

We measure time by my voice on the old wire recorder:
"I'm too tiwerd to sing," my three year old self
tells my mother. "Say kaka baby," my mother begs.
My father sings, "Thanks for the memories."

By the frazzled leather web
of a Spalding fielder's mitt
that insured a ball's nonstop flight
and much happiness for batters.

By a Ludwig Oyster Pearl drum set,
with dusty Zildjian cymbals
on my third floor, kick beats and
rim shots locked inside calfskin
membranes and creviced in silent
splintered drumsticks—totems to
Temptations, Vandellas, Supremes.

By Allen Ginsberg chanting "Om"
in Lincoln Park spreading Buddha-calm
while the whole world watched.

By reciting, "Being to timelessness
as it's to time"[2] to each other
on a mountaintop in Gold Hill Colorado
forty-three years ago—a bottle
of champagne still in our liquor cabinet

though neither of us drinks anymore.

Or the day, once a year, when we replay
your water breaking, my sitting up
straight in bed, your uterus unwilling,
the C-section, the nurse saying,
"It's a boy."

Last Moments

It will be like any other night
only there will be

no reason to water the plants
or shop for food

or dog-ear a novel page.
It will be a snowy winter's night

on Walloon lake, my hospital bed
pressed against the picture window.

I'll miss the snow on my face,
the mystery of frozen water.

Or mid-sentence my head will smack
the dinner table like a dead fish

slapped against a dock. Or they'll hear
my wheezes down a nursing home hall:

I will count my breaths until
I get to *número el fin.*

Will I think of how lucky I was at love?
The score at the bottom of the ninth?

Why there was something rather than nothing?
Or how there weren't any clear answers?

II

Bathroom Bill

The south has risen again
to this new low. The latest etiolation
from a chronically fusty population.

Bathroom Bill, in North Carolina, says,
"If y'all is transgendered, ya caint
use a potty sept ta one
you was born to." Ole' Bathroom Bill,
ten gallon dome, six gun and spurs,
a chap with chaps, will be a guardin'
them latrines, yessir! Bill and his posse,
Gabby, the Genital Inspector,
Pete, Chief of the Pudenda Police,
and Cassidy, commandin' the Commode
Cops and all their sub-genital inspectors
on privy patrol will insure
only pure born birthers use bathrooms
in North Carolina.

Bathroom Bill is sweatin'
over how that thar inspectin'
is gonna go. He paces, kicks the dirt,
and askes his horse if they is gonna
have to make people show
their buckskins, their saddlebags—
if ya catch his meanin'. Shucks,
he ain't never done nothing like
this before. Nosir! This here
is one of them search and seizures
that could cause a seizure.
Then whart? Are they gonna
have to pack tongue blades
along with their Colt 45s?
Gawl darnit!
Caint all them North Carolina

lawyers and congressmen
go to the bathroom
by them lonesome selves
and leave ole' Bathroom Bill
to his pony, his jerky,
and his designer potty?

Election 2016

Our hundred foot oak

>   stately for so long as we could remember
>   governed our backyard with the kindness
>
>   of gnarled branches that spread gifts
>   of shade in summer, stark strength in winter.

Our oak that withstood

>   fence construction
>   ivy infestation
>
>   generations of kids who climbed its bark
>   and swung from its sturdy limbs.

Our oak that survived and endured

>   vicious varieties of Zephyrus' wrath:
>   scathing sun, freezing rain,
>
>   dilating and contracting water
>   under its woody skin.

Our lovely oak lost two huge branches,

>   one calm and cloudless afternoon,
>   that fell on our old bent locust tree;
>
>   like a forest of dominoes that locust
>   collapsed, in turn, on our house.

Our ancient oak that had given us

      so much turned out to be rotten inside,
      a master of backyard trumpery, those torn

      limbs revealed an empty inner core that
      left no choice but to take it down.

Our precious oak gave way to the tree man's

      spiked boots that gripped her creviced derma.
      Chainsaw buzz dug into my soul's flesh

      while her severed and noosed limbs
      were lowered to the ground.

Our oak was no more.

      We were left with scorched earth,
      a parched and crooked swale,

      a hollow stump out of which
      nothing could grow.

Happy New Year

January 2, 2017 and I go shopping
at the Giant Eagle in Edgewood.
I buy enough groceries for
the 65 million who didn't vote
for Trump, and check out in Adriana's line.
I ask this lovely black woman,
her eyes like languid pools,
how she's doing. Not good, she says,
someone stole her wallet the day
before Christmas with all her credit
cards and ID and overdrew her bank
account by $185 dollars. The worst
is that her wallet was lifted
in the bathroom of Giant Eagle
where she works. Her eyes
now two cloud-covered moons.
I'm sorry, I say, but it will pass
and tell her that, years ago, my
wallet was stolen from the front seat
of my car where I'd left it after
I dropped off our son at the airport
for his first trip away to college.
Evidently my heart and most
of my brain flew off with him.
I might as well have put a sign
on the wallet that said Here,
Steal Me, which makes Adriana
laugh, and I am happy to give
her a little New Year's cheer.
On the way out of Giant Eagle
I pass a middle-aged couple.
The woman says to her man,
You took a long-ass mother fuckin' nap—
twelve hours! No, he replies,
and shakes his head like a wet dog.

Yes, says his woman, a long-ass
mother fuckin' nap. I think
of all those who stayed home
during our last election
and didn't vote. I think
of what that long-ass mother-
fuckin' nap cost us all.

Office

Of·fice (ô fĭs, ŏf ĭs): n. 1. A room with
four walls, sometimes in the shape
of an oval, that usually contains
a desk and other materials
for conducting business.

Example: In January, 2009, Barack Obama
walked into the Oval Office
knowing that his job
was to care for and love
his country in the way
he cared for and loved
his wife, Michelle,
and their two daughters;
eight years later
he walked into history
having achieved that goal.

2. A political post, either elected,
appointed, or ordained.

Example: President Obama brought
to the office of the president
dignity and grace—the imprimatur
of kindness, compassion,
and wisdom.

3. A prayerful rite and/or ritualized prayer
performed by clergy or other religions persons.

Example: The berobed monk folds
his hands above his purfled cuffs
and prays that his country
won't be transformed into
a hateful place where men brag

about molesting women, make fun
of handicapped people, humiliate
the parents of a Muslim man
who gave his life for his country,
ban Muslims from entering the United States
because they are Muslims, build
a Soviet-style wall of shame
on its southern border, make
it impossible for sick people
to get insurance, receive chemotherapy,
or endure illness without bankruptcy,
and would never, ever, ridicule a man
whose jaw is still mangled and misshapen
from beatings he took at the hands
of white racists in Selma Alabama.

Antonyms:

1. Gold-gilded lobby of a babbling tower in Manhattan

2. Jingoistic self-aggrandizing right wing propaganda rallies

3. Vituperative, narcissistic, obsessional tweeting that embarrasses the country

The March

Using The Washington Post's (January 20, 2017) list of
27 words never before used in an inaugural address.[3]

We bleed freedom,
the unstoppable potion
against the promised windswept landscape
of stolen and unrealized dreams,
of depletion and disrepair;
against the carnage he proposes:
stealing healthcare from millions
while procuring trillions
for a subsidized oil industry,
turning disagreements into rusted
tombstones of political cant,
waging a sad war against
millions of Islamic believers
for the misguided violence
of a few.

Flush with lady liberty
we march in solidarity
with the vast sprawl of humanity
who still believe in kindness,
in the untapped compassion within,
and with those who honor
our urban siblings trapped
in the trammels of poverty.

Here and overseas freedom's
people tunnel into the infrastructure
of justice, and celebrate virtue
ripped from a tyrant's digits.

Floating Landscapes

After a painting by Karen Cappatto

In Izmir life jackets fill windows of clothing stores.
Faces are gabled by tears and veils. Wizened hands
shelter then pass a pale child against a pale sky.
Will you love him? Will you make a place for her?
Love leaps above the world over landscapes of freedom.
If the land is legal, if our surfaces are *at large*,
how could children have become illegal?

The routes we navigate to get to each other,
that network of us, floats in our world. We sail,
swim, splash, tread—connect, become I,
become thou, yearn for invitation, gladly
accept it when offered and when not…
our world drowns before we do.

We, privileged, have arrived safely, but safety floats.
We landed ones swim, but don't know it.
We are refugees from the wayward breeze,
the ocean of I-don't-belong.
It's not a matter of opening our arms,
benevolence, even kindness.
It's navigating our floating landscape—
the land upon which we all sail.

Wisdom

Wisdom is an albatross
living in Midway Atoll
National Wildlife Refuge.
She's sixty-six years old,
my age, and is nesting
an egg, a new life,
hope in a shell.

On the front page of the Times
a photo, today, of a man
who carries a bundle
in his left arm—
a child wrapped in a beige
and brown blanket with
fawn spots decorating
its cover. In his right hand
he holds a plastic bag
connected to IV tubing that winds
from the bag and disappears
into the doe-brindled bundle.

Behind him a veiled woman.
Worry folds her hijab
as clearly as the squint
of the man's eyes
or his lips' purse.
He grasps the future,
a damaged package
cradled in his arm.
They flee a landscape
strewn with tyranny's
detritus called Aleppo.

Wisdom is an albatross
sitting on an egg
in Midway Atoll.
Our government there
has pledged
to protect her.

Embrace

The human heart pumps
        100 CCs of blood at a time
        and that's how much it holds
        when it stops

We measure everything except
        the grief of a daughter whose father,
        Fethi Sekin, was killed by a car bomb
        in Izmir last week

Killed by some zealot who thought
        he'd save Turkey or purify Islam
        or purchase his way into heaven
        with Fethi Sekin's 100 CCs

But the photo in today's paper is
        of Mr. Sekin's 8 year old daughter
        who does to his coffin what she wants
        to do to her daddy

She hugs it, lays her head
        against its flag-draped contour,
        and dreams of the times
        they'll never have

Safe At Home
For Malik Hamilton

Last night, Andrew McCutchen, "Cutch" to us, slammed a tough one
into right field that hopped happily over Minnesota's Eddie Rosario's
left shoulder and dribbled onto the wall where Rosario, like the lame god
Hephaestus, took his sweet time retrieving the orb, while Cutch,
speedy as Apollo's chariot, rounded third base and smashed into
the Twin's Mount Olympus in the earthly form of Edwardo Nunez.

Their collision made the Hadron Collider blush and set the Richter Scale
thumping. The men who used to be in blue, but are now in gray,
called interference on Mount Olympus and sent our Pittsburgh Apollo
to the safety of home plate. Later, Cutch made poetry of the event,
"Definitely a foul there," he said. "Fifteen yard penalty, roughing the passer,
automatic first down." Andrew, our passer, was safe at home,

as I hope he is tonight and all the nights of his young life. I hope
he avoids the men in black who threw Eric Garner, Samuel Dubose,
Jonny Gammage, Walter Scott, John Crawford III, Dontre Hamilton,
and so many African American men out of the game forever,
out before they got to third base—passers, under
the lights of this long American night.

The Ur-Money Shot

I wanted to touch the big cop's gun, wanted
to run my fingers along its hard black handle.

Oh what my former psychoanalyst colleagues
would have done with that fantasy!

Both my former analysts would have loved it,
would have made thousands of dollars off of it,

would have provided weekend pot puffing moola
for their little darlings at college.

My first analyst often bragged about how well he and his wife
had raised their three boys—always

in contrast to how we were raising our son. When I became an analyst
I chanced to overhear his soricine wife blab that their oldest boy

had got their youngest son addicted to "the mary wanna." I got to hear
my old analyst say, "Now Barbara, let's don't tell all the family secrets."

Back to me wanting to touch the cop's gun: my fantasy
was crushed by the thought that he would shoot me

should I touch his gun—still a fantasy, I know, the Ur-Money Shot,
I know—but then I remembered that I'm white.

He wouldn't shoot me, only beat me with his long black baton—
another fantasy, I know. The racial point, the real point:

that black men are official targets in this country, is not a fantasy,
is beyond my former colleagues, irreducible to

their grizzled theoretical slipstream. Over a hundred years
of psychotherapy and we are left with this.

Forward Pass

So he couldn't stand the anthem

Sat down for Sandra Bland, Eric Garner, Samuel Dubose, Jonny Gammage,
    Walter Scott, John Crawford III, Dontre Hamilton, and all the others

   Gunned down

   Terrified to suicide

Because no matter how much money he makes

He'll still have to tell his kids

   To keep their hands up

   Keep them visible

   Say Yes sir No sir to the white man

   With the badge

   With the gun

Because selling cigarettes
Changing lanes without signaling
Driving a Jaguar while black
Walking home to grandpa are

Capital offenses these days

   Days where dignity sits on the sidelines

Colin Kaepernick completed a forward pass

   Wouldn't stand on freedom's gallows

The Lame God

After #11, a drawing by Rick Claraval

The lame god watched
the great Greek hero
carry the torch. Crippled
from the start, Hephaestus,
too, wanted *arétē*. Still

he stood on Olympus,
watched Achilles drag Hector
round the city gates,
watched Odysseus and his son
hang all the girls who serviced
Penelope's suiters,

watched the torch light up
Western Civilization with
the virtues of violence,
retribution, and revenge.
Had they but limped

into eternity, like Hephaestus,
taken that magnificent left turn,
metamorphosed into something
humane, the word *hero*

would mean kindness, tolerance—
would torch the world with
the blue and brilliant
light of peace.

Chagall

Blessed in sunglow, surrounded by six of his stained glass panels,
      bathed in a prism of brilliance.

     Was he a surrealist?

     A cubist?

Mostly he was a Russian Jew bathed in exhausted crimson Shabbat nights,
or cloaked in the monochromatic strength of a prayer shawl.

Mostly he floated above the world where love met dismay,
      and the view, the view spread over his dreamscape

through gentle, through bloody, through inversion, through invasion,
      through crucifixion.

The last "savior" brought two thousand years of strife.

What's next?

Who will light our candles? Pound our nails?

A disembodied cow's head?

A flaming fish playing a fiddle?

The Persistence of Memory

Dali made me late for everything,
made me never think of my age,
made me frame time as
a mess of melted clocks.

Memory persists, pushes, penetrates—
hallucinates the past that lives in
the future, the now that is always then,
always soon to be. Still

it is those fey atoms of biology, our
cells, that imprison us in time. All
the philosophers on the planet can't
stop that final moment's approach—

the moment those clocks reconstitute,
drip by drip, and stop.

En Passant

From a series of photographs by Jake Reinhart

I.

On the hanger
its shoulders droop,
an empty avatar
of his being.
He wore that jacket
when he raked
leaves. It was his fall
cloak. He cut a strapping
figure—long black pipe
jutting from his mouth
against the moldy mound
he set ablaze when
he was done. That smell
told our lives.

II.

The new people painted
the wall where he hung
his jacket. Mom held onto
that coat until the day
we carried her away.
It still held his smell,
even if she alone
could detect it.

III.

Now he dwells in a frame.
He was a Marine.
Semper Fidelis he'd say
and kiss mom. He never
spoke about the war.

IV.

Sycamore shadows splay
across the garage door—
tesserae of light
behind which he
kept the rake along with
his other tools.

V.

Mom holds his picture
in a frame of her
holding his picture.
The paint on the front
railing is chipped. The new
people haven't gotten
to it yet.

Toothbrushes

I listen today, October 27, 2016, to an interview
with Sylvia Plath on what would have been
her eighty-fourth birthday had she not plunged
her head into a cold oven and turned on

those despairing fumes. In the interview
she said she couldn't squeeze toothbrushes
into a poem, a reason to write prose,
she said. Her voice was full

of energy and hope. She sounded like
a lovely person. I bet her teeth were
white as the finest porcelain. I bet she had
a quality toothbrush with firm bristles

with which she carefully brushed,
three times on her uppers and lowers,
making sure to reach behind molars
to get crumbs of breakfast toast.

I bet she loved the sound of scrubbing
her toothbrush made against those
pearly protrusions that churlish Ted liked
to tongue. She surely enjoyed the purling

rinse from faucet to mouth, the splash
of sputum in the sink, the soft click
of brush against glass when she
put it to sleep for the night.

She must have relished the fresh taste,
that minty zing, the rebirth toothpaste
promises even at the end of day. What
if Sylvia Plath had put toothbrushes

into one of her poems, had celebrated those monuments to the quotidian, honored the bristly minutia that hallow the everyday, that augur the promise of tomorrow? What if?

Endurance

Based on "The Prison of my Youth,"
a sculpture by Rick Claraval

Caged within his father's words—
"You're worthless," "Shut your mouth,"
"You don't know nothin', boy."
"Why are you so stupid, boy?"

Shame bolts pierced everything
that made him. Cylinder of hate
created by his creator:
la parole that imprisons,

a tropic doom chrysalis that
became *la langue*, the system
his preformed body writhed
within, the skin of his dreams,

filleted by sound chisels,
a genetic code of conflict,
never escaped but evolved
into art, a metamorphosis

of triumph—what separates us
from animals and from parents
who act like animals.

Farther

How strange to watch through my hand
the afternoon light patch on my porch.
I'm disappearing as I write. I sip
Diet Pepsi, watch its dark fizzle trickle
down my esophagus and drain
into my tummy. The imaginary is

so weightless. I'm beyond ether now.
Subatomic and unapologetic I've become
the Higgs Field, host to interstellar baseball.
Here comes an ion. I'll swat that baby
out of the park, out of every park.
I'll swat the park out of the park.

In second grade the nun showed my mother
a drawing I'd made of my father. I spelled
father *farther.* Even then I had an unconscious.
Now that I'm cosmological, the invisible
field that gives matter its charge, I'll find
him out there … farther … my father … farther.
How much will I charge him, and with what?

While briefly a star I did not collapse
into a black hole, never lost my light
in a singularity. I am not now, nor was I ever,
so dense as to be the size of a sugar cube,
packed so tightly I'd have to explode.

Casino

She stands beside him
He pulls the levers
He punches the buttons

She watches as the icons don't match
She shifts from one foot to the other
He pulls the lever again

The symbols don't match
His paycheck is almost gone
He punches the buttons

His paycheck is gone
In their pickup
She hands him half

The cheese and cracker package
She brought with her
They share the lonely can

Of beer from the cooler
She wonders how they will
Pay for gas on the drive home

Whether the sitter will understand
Or the kids complain about
The powdered milk on the cornflakes

That night she humps him back
While he's on top of her
She will never leave him

Hombre Y Compadre

This round brown man, brown no more, yellow from jaundice.

I practice my Spanish on him, the little I have when at Denver General,
        my clean white Hospital Attendant uniform,
        my name tag with the HA after it—
        the only credential I have for years.

This yellow brown man's swollen abdomen,
        the look of *embarazo* like all the alcoholics,
        but this man glossed with the soft sheen of friendship.

Each time he was admitted I called him *mi compadre*.
        No matter how sick, he'd smile, *Si, mi compadre*, he'd repeat.

        I'm not there when he dies.

Phil, my colleague and, like me, a conscious objector working
        at Denver General Hospital in 1970, took him to the morgue.

        These are morgue days.

Phil gets angry at the alcoholics. I know what he means.
        It's hard to watch these guys come to our ward over and over again
        until there is no again.

My father drank and smoked himself to death so I pulse, nod, wrap myself in
        a blanket, ride a horse in the snow when they die.

During his last hospitalization I briefly forget the word for friend
        and call him *hombre*.

Compadre, he quickly corrects me, and settles, with my help,
        into the cool sheets.

The Return

After "The Lonely Nepenthes Sumagaya" a glass sculpture
by Bronwen Hellman

Freed from its chrysalis
it flew away and left
its vacant home
to decay and scrape
over leaves and thistle,
hedge and grass,
whistle in the wind,
caressed by smells
of putrification—
sweet life-giving
aromas of death.

What leaves returns,
becomes a vole's home,
a nest for barn sparrows,
red-winged blackbirds,
and grackles.

On Townsend Road
the dead deer feeds
coyotes and condors,
a lone mourning dove
stands beside its fallen mate.
We can't understand its grief.
We can't understand
anything's grief.

The Merciful Beneficence of Repression

Let's just say the incense fell out of his censer
a long time ago. Let's just say his holy water boat sunk.

Let's just say his rosary beads bounced wildly along his psyche
and dribbled onto the sanctuary floor. No one wanted to serve

mass with Monsignor Hartman. He would grab your arm in an iron grip
and grimace—as close as he got to love. But here I was, alone, serving

a requiem mass for a poor young woman who died of a church and state
enforced coat hanger abortion. Her relations wailed and keened—

one of them crawled on her knees up the center aisle of St. Mary's
where Monsignor Hartman and I stood before the small casket.

Because the other two altar boys had fagged out, I had to balance
the censer and holy water boat, the charcoal and incense while

Monsignor, in his black cape and mood, stared at me maliciously
until I offered him the holy water. He took the aspergillum

and stepped down to anoint the coffin with the church's holy tears.
Instead he dropped the aspergillum and grabbed his throat,

his pallor as pale as back-alley putty, blessed *terra* of terror. "Holy
shit!" I intoned. Was the old blowhard having a heart attack?

The grieving multitude gasped. What possessed me to look at my feet
I don't recall. Head bowed, I discovered my right shoe planted atop

Monsignor's cape causing the gold clasp at his throat to smite his Adam's
Apple. "Holy shit!" I blurted again and lifted my foot.

The old man winged toward the casket like an ecclesiastical trapeze flyer.
I remember nothing after that except the image of Monsignor Hartman draped

over the coffin, clutching it like a vulture in a Caravaggio nightmare—
my first experience of the merciful beneficence of repression.

Follow Me

Pat was a talker. Today we'd say
he had ADHD, but back then
he was just a talker. Sr. Dinardo often
told him to stop talking, but he couldn't.

She put his desk in a corner and
forbade us to talk to Pat so far away,
by himself, in the back of our room.
Desperate for interaction he took

to bouncing in his chair past his desk—
an attempt to join us in egregious defiance
of Sister. Clearly he was seven-year-old evil.
One day, Pat bucked his chair again.

This time Sr. Dinardo summoned him
to the front of the class. Maybe
he would join us now, could be one
of us again. "Follow me," she said,

in imitation, no doubt, of her husband,
our Lord and savior. Gone ten minutes,
we were anxious—left alone so long.
When she led him back into our room

she had put him in a pink dress,
pink girl shoes on his feet, pink
bows tied to each arm. When
the bell rang for recess, Sr. Dinardo

made Pat join us on the playground
where grades one through five
swarmed and frenzied. In our
second grade classroom,

Sr. Dinardo taught us to discern
minor from major chords, the pitch
when notes rose or fell, talents
I still retain and treasure.

Drumbeat

Kids from the high school band were demonstrating instruments in our
     fourth grade classroom.

I liked the trumpet best, but I became a drummer because "drum" was the only
     instrument I was sure I could spell.

Mr. Cribelli, our band director, taught me the double stroke roll. I still remember
     the thrill when my dat dat / dat dat / dat dat / dat dat
     became drrrrrrrrrrrrrrrrrrrrrrrrrrrrrrrrrrrr!

I remember my first snare drum—a Ludwig Blue Sparkle that I played in my
     basement along with the records of Pete Fountain and Al Hirt.

When The Beatles arrived my parents bought me a cheap orange spackled
     Japanese drum kit with cymbals that sounded like tin cans.

No matter: Greg Wall, Joe Risha, and I formed a rock band and were hired by the
     Cheyenne Country Club to play our first and last gig.

We only had three songs: "Louie Louie," "Blue Moon," and "Wipeout!"
     We played them for four hours.

Someone would make a request: "Can you play 'Twist and Shout'
     by The Beatles?" Sure, we'd say, and play "Wipeout!"

Another would ask, "Can you play 'I Want to Hold Your Hand?'" Of course,
     we'd smile, and play "Louie Louie."

When I was 16 I played drums in a Soul Band: The Kansas City Soul Association,
     although we were all based in Cheyenne. We were

four black singers and four white musicians who shared cigarettes and drank
     out of each other's Coke cans, broke all those racist rules.

We made tremendous amounts of money. I bought a Ludwig Oyster Pearl
   drum set with Zildjian cymbals, the exact kit that Ringo played.

I had it paid for two months before it arrived at Cross Music in Cheyenne—
   $880 in 1966!

Two years later we came in second at the KIMN Battle of the Bands in Denve
   (they weren't about to let a band with black singers get first place).

On stage that night, Flip, our lead singer, fell to his knees, "Please Please Please
   he sang—James Brown style.

I thought I heard the tinny whine of amplifier feedback, but it was the screams
   of girls and women who had pressed themselves up against the stage.
   Policemen escorted us off the stage that day, our day of fame.

Years later, my wife and I were leaving Denver for a new life in Pittsburgh,
   she as a psychiatrist, I as a graduate student in psychology.

I thought I'd sell my drums, too sophisticated now for my musical past.
   The night I advertised my Ludwig Oyster Pearl for sale in the paper,

I dreamt that I was serving a requiem mass at St. Mary's in Cheyenne. The bla
   caped priest and I led the casket up the aisle to the communion rail

where I opened the casket to look at the deceased and found my drums
   lying there, ready to face eternity.

Now my drums preside over my music room on the third floor of our home. A
   I play them—they still Please Please Please.

Pawn Shop

Drum sets in the window, dusty
cynosures that pull me toward the store.
A scatter of dining room chairs block
the entrance, a bereft world that impedes
access, like a shattered Serra sculpture.

(Who no longer sits on those chairs,
smells the Sunday roast,
plays Wednesday night poker,
does her geometry homework
at the table after school?)

Failure's fragrance pervades the place.
I pass shelves of gnarled garden
tools, smelly old fashioned suitcases,
cracked CD cases, moldy paperbacks—
bestsellers gone to seed. I pass

soundless trumpets and saxophones, chipped
statues of emptiness, monuments to loneliness,
forgotten wrist watches unwound by time,
knives scabrous and prosaic under glass.
I finally get to those windowed traps,

chrome plating cracked with rust,
bass and toms feckless and skint as their
battered owners—rimshot silenced by
smack-soaked skins and cymbals
lovingly stroked, once, with hope.

Antiques

For Art Hanscum

Mother ran through our house
with a hammer, wide-eyed, wild,
attacked our front door as if it was
a wooden rapist. Medusa hair,

snake pit in motion, she slammed
the hammer down, over and over,
"antiquing" our open door. Art and I felt
the chill. Cheyenne hit 20 below

that day cancelling school, warming
our 16 year old hearts. The radio warned
that exposed skin would freeze in five
minutes so Art threw on a jacket and

walked the mile to our house, happy
to beat the odds, as he beat me
at endless games of chess and gin
rummy that day. Ma finally finished

off the door and brought her madness
down upon an innocent chest in our garage.
Art and I hadn't known that an antique
was a piece of furniture pounded

into submission then spray painted
with a godawful smelling copper
goo. We thought it was something
old, like we are now. Me a bald,

fat, greybeard in Pittsburgh; Art in
Florida, pummeled by Parkinson's
Disease, still able to clobber my ass
at chess and gin rummy.

Put Them All Together (with stage directions)

(sing to the melody of the soppy Irish song M-O-T-H-E-R)

M stands for the murderous feelings you had for my father,
        wishing him dead the day before
        he died from a heart attack.

O stands for the ostracism you endured after you attacked
        me with a broom and I didn't speak to you for a year in the eighties.

T is for the trial you put me through when I brought Judy, my Jewish girlfriend,
        home to meet you and you bragged how you had "Jewed-down"
        Mexican merchants on a trip to Tijuana.

H is for the humiliation I felt as you boasted to your friends
        that I wore "Husky" pants when I weighed 164 pounds
        in sixth grade and you didn't think I was fat.

E stands for the psychotic envy you displayed when, in your seventies,
        you proclaimed that you were "prettier" than me.

R is for your favorite name for my father: "Rotten Son-of-a-Bitch,"
        which you called him when he was drunk and didn't care.

(stop singing)

Put them all together and they spell … regret.

They spell … I loved you anyway.

They spell … I'm glad you're out of your misery.

They spell … it couldn't have been otherwise.

III

Denial

Float down De Nile down
the psychoanalytic Lethe

Dial back the shame
Dial up the shaman

Magical reality
of a drowned polysemy

Forget

Nail down
the den that ails

Who but the inventor of denial could claim that a patient with several feet of
    gauze left in her nose was hysterically bleeding

Or blow smoke rings of no consequences
from twenty cigars a day

Freud's psyche was an ameba
whose pseudopodia
encircled the world

There was no other

Repression

Freud's shirts
starched stiff
arrested attire
his dickey
erect and shiny

Press on the pleasure
Refry desire
Stoke the Freudian fire

Repress son
prodigal boy
always returns

It was supposed to be about liberation but turned out to be about how unfree
      freedom is

Early on Freud pressed on
the foreheads of his patients
forcing down what they'd exposed

Freud's trousers
stood by themselves at night
like a fireman's outfit

Freud slid down the panic pole
to rescue us from
what we didn't know

proved once again
what was erect
eventually falls

Those cigars
a caesura in the preconscious
precancerous mouth

a vagina dentata that analytic floss
can't repair or prevent
An opera of operations

A prosthetic jaw that made
the professor whistle when he spoke
So he rarely uttered a sound

which caused his American sycophants to ape
a gaping analytic silence

What they thought was psychoanalytic technique
was actually the old man's vanity

Rationalization

The man behind the couch
serves libido for lunch

destrudo for dinner
Mmmmmmmmmm

Ration your reason
Your ratio of reality
Too much is scary

He should get paid for missed sessions
He has kids you need to send to college
A mortgage to pay with your neurosis

That's understandable

A good gig if you can get it
And I got it when I entered
the Psychoanalytic Institute in 1990

My Supervising Analyst charged me $180 an hour on a patient I was seeing
for $10 an hour four times a week

Es vas reasonable

I was only in the hole $140 a week
for the privilege of my supervisor falling asleep
while I was reporting to him
my patient's dream

He wanted to empathize with that dream
by dreaming himself

He lived in a huge house
with oak paneling
oriental rugs
crystal

He should get my money
He had a right to it
He was rational

Projection

It's either spring or it's not
Michael Dickman

You are dumb to tell your life
Utterly dumb you(r) utter
On the couch

Only he knows
He's the pro

Only he can swim in your stream

Your unctions are extreme

This project of all projects depends upon your projection onto your analyst
      of your competence

You anoint him

You(')r(e) tense

That last anointing
So annoying
False spring

Frozen death of buds

Identification

Freud said Grow a beard
and beards sprang from the cheeks
and chins of analysts
as if they'd put seeds
in their mouths

Freud said Light up your cigars
and the American Psychoanalytic Association
became a tsunami of smoke

Freud said Sit in a chair behind a couch and the army of analysts like race
    car drivers at the Grand Prix ran toward their consulting rooms and
    assumed their positions

Freud said Say very little to your patients
Make lots of money
Start every paper you write
with some quote from something I've written
no matter how obscure

Freud said If you love me
wear these rings
in memory of me

Lacan said Make it as difficult as you can

Lacan said Use the conditional voice
Write and speak dramatically
hysterically

After all we are the country of Charcot

Lacan said Listen to me fart in public

Lacan said If you love me

you will speak like me
dress like me
fart like me

Anna Freud said Expel Lacan he's a charlatan
and the International Psychoanalytical Association expelled Lacan

Anna Freud said As analysts we are not concerned
with the events in the external world as such
but only with their repercussions in the mind

So much for the Holocaust
which generations of analysts
ignored when dealing with their Jewish analysands

Stolorow said that he invented the word "intersubjectivity"
while drinking a pitcher of beer
with a pal in California

Scores of sycophants
who hadn't read anything but psych books
believed him

Before them all Wilhelm Fleiss told Freud
It's all in the nose

He knows said Freud

A foot and a half of gauze left in Emma Eckstein's nose

Someone in Denmark knows

Regression

Repeal reason
License aggression

Freeze to death
Burn to death

Trump or Rubio
Steele magnolias or cheerios

There's nothing to choose
Well there's Cruz

      Let's turn our country into a church

We've gone from
the gleaming city cresting a hill
to polymorphous perversity
pounds of religious swill

From Lincoln telling Douglas
      "When a man hears himself somewhat misrepresented, it provokes
      him,—at least I find it so with myself; but when misrepresentation
      becomes very gross and palpable, it is apt to amuse him"

To Trump saying of Rubio
      "I wanted to show the size of my hands, how I could grab him. I
      could grab him. I could grab that guy like nothing"

Trope a dope

Let's have a hand for the penis

Let's go back to Junior High
to third grade
to the sand pile

Stick our heads in aggression

Let's elect regression

Displacement/Sublimation

What place is dis

How sublime sublimation

Chain gang a workin' along Displacement Road

for the sub/bureau the psychoanalytic precinct

Sublimation or displacement

Kicking a dog after the iconic rough day or painting the Sistine ceiling
        because it's forbidden to be gay

The place you're
meant to be
bumped along
the metonymic
highway

Yield the right of way

Yield the right way

Isolation of Affect

Sequester senses
Exile empathy
Ghettoize guts
Sterilize sensation
Neutralize nerves

Blank that slate

The patient sat in front of us
exposed on a stage
at the Big Psychiatric Hospital

Not so Grand Rounds

In one year's time
Her father   husband   daughter
dead   destroyed
one way or another

She had only herself and whatever endings there were to her nerves

What a learning experience

The senior analyst whom we candidates were there to watch interview this pati
remained silent

Not a gesture or a nod
much less a *sorry for your loss*

My supervisor was thrilled
He didn't give in to the empathy crowd
to the compassion cabal she chortled

If you have feelings when with your patient
You need another analysis

It's isolation we're after
Lot's wife and Eurydice

Don't falter

Seven Variations on a Buddha Shove

I

A man skids to the cliff's ledge
After him   a tiger

He looks down
Another tiger on the canyon floor

He must jump
He jumps

Grasps a vine on the way down
Dangles on cliff's edge

Two mice appear
One white
One black
Gnaw on the vine

Gnaw on the vine with truculence

The man spies a strawberry bush barely within reach
He grabs a strawberry
Eats it

Luscious!

II

Tiger-breath bakes his calves
Thighs simmer
Toes cramp against the ledge

Are his shoes too small?

Wind whips his body
Vine furrows bloody his palm

Thick and sticky
Rotator cuff tears   like a tooth yanked with pliers

Legs flail like a noosed man
Tiger-breath chrysalis steams his torso

Mice torture and tweak
Fungible
Like night   like day

Pained strain for the strawberry

Tongue scrapes rough fruity ridges
Teeth squeeze
Tingle tease

Sweet juice soulburst!

III

Paws pound the ground like bass drums
Bouncing tympani
Mothers of thunder

His wheezes asthma the forest floor

Below

Toothy pre-crunch requiem
Ravenous roar

Wind buzz
Wind whirl

Hand-skin rips like a butcher's slice
Rotator cuff pops like a firecracker in a beer can

Lips slurp sweet strawberry nectar

Tongue-suck jails the juice

His smile sounds like a smile!

IV

Olfactory offal terror reek
Predation musk
Perfume of prey

Acrid attar of lion-breath
Smell of blood

Dust

Dirt

Torn flesh and vine stink

Strawberry scent

Aroma of here
Aroma of now!

V

Acid
Vomit
Salt
Spitless tongue

Strawberry sugarburst

Sweet saliva syrup
A little tart   but in a good way

Palate of calm!

VI

His world in a hospital bed
Her face sweaty marble

She's not going to make it

Every vein pulses
A tsunami of dread

Breathless   death
After him   waits

For us all

He leaps   grasps

Days into nights into days into nights into days

Thick tongue mouth sear
Dangling between panic and despair

Forty years married he
Bends towards her face
The edge of peace

Kisses her lips

Luscious!

VII

He didn't see it coming
But knew it was there
Engine roar
Metal and glass

Crash

He holds on   just barely
Respirator moves up and down
Up and down

Something gnaws
Life flakes asunder like scurf

An owl blinks and flies away

Heart pounds sputters
Threads into either

Stops

Monitor's plangent monotonous song

He thinks that kiss
He thinks her breath

Sweet!

The Unomnific Collapse of the Universe

1. The Argument

It breasted us all:
capped, burned, plugged
the ground like a blazing
plastic umbilical cord

at molten earth center.
If we uncapped that pipe,
we'd set off the Big Unbang,
the unomnific flaming collapse of the Universe.

Densely packed inferno
simmering sugar cube:
the burning white-capped pipe
up against the smoldering cabin wall.

2. Imbued with Fire and Awe

It breasted us all—
the ground,
a burning plastic umbilical
must molten earth together.
We, at earth's roiling center,
the Big Unbang
retro-omnific flaming universe
packed inferno
baking minor chord anti-Zarathustra
capped pipe simmering sugar cube
against the smoldering cabin—

Oh wow!

3. Interrogated and Mocked

It breasted us all?
How big were they?
Like a burning plastic umbilical
prematurely cut,
we, at the fiery earth,
measured in centigrade and Fahrenheit
the Big Unbang?
How would you know, smarty pants?
We backed into the packed inferno!
Is the party over?
Simmering sugar cube—
where you stored your acid?

Oh wow, or was it far out?

Ten Jazz Standards

1. *I Mean You*

Don't look around
I'm talkin' to you

2. *How Insensitive*

On line all day
Hoping to get offended

3. *Alone Together*

You thought we were friends
We weren't

4. *A Child Is Born*

Every time you open your mouth

5. *Come Rain Or Come Shine*

You are so predictable
Liver flukes are more interesting

6. *Autumn Leaves*

Why won't you

7. *Take The A Train*

It's for a-holes

8. *Day Dream*

Any dream
Is better than listening to you

9. *In A Sentimental Mood*

You hated sentimentality
Something no one will ever feel for you

10. *How Deep Is The Ocean*

Why don't you jump in and find out?

Ten Paintings by Matisse

1. *The Open Window*

    iron bars

2. *Blue Nude*

    aren't they all

3. *The Conversation*

    strictly one-sided

4. *The Painter and His Model*

    were one and the same

    always

5. *Woman with a Hat*

    spits at Carole Maso

    steals her *cahier*

6. *Bathers with a Turtle*

    those motherfuckers

    he was just a turtle

    out for a swim

7. *Beasts of the Sea*

    ask Churchill

8. *The Music Lesson*

    slap my fingers again

    bitch

9. *Male Nude*

    age 27

    they found water

    in his lungs

10. *Luxury, Calm, and Desire*

    set out the juice glass

    watch the bees drown

    we have time

THINGS THAT COME IN WAVES[4]

I. X Rays, Gamma Rays, Microwaves, MRIs
How deep must we go—
past skin, past bone, past muscle?
Descartes thought the soul resided
in the Pineal gland.
A pea-shaped bleb of light
cleaves to something anterior,
or caudle, or posterior.
Eventually we are all read-out
by someone in a white jacket
we don't know; a stranger who,
between a sip of diet soda
and a bite of peanut butter bread,

counts the peaks and troughs—
calculates the dead.

II. The Gravitational Harmonies of Deep Space
We were never a beginning, only
the other side of a collapsed star,
black hole excreta; random
whim of an indifferent singularity.
The Big Bang: the next feature
after a celestial intermission
between a gazillion cosmic films,
an astrocinematic ructus
with no beginning, no final act.
Only we end, eventually
not even a mote bowered
in some defunct god's eye.

Our son, his world, my wife's hand,
my myopic Everland.

III. Sound

That finds itself
then gets lost
finds itself
becomes confused
drops into splendid solitude.
Goldberg Variation number twenty five
deliquescent embryo come alive
but barely so—
the question, *will it survive*,
lingers throughout.
Glenn Gould's hum carries Bach's song
to its refulgent end.

We strive to grasp its meaning.
It eludes us now, then, and again.

IV. Weather Fronts

It can get so cold
that your soul turns to frost
like rime around a cocktail glass;
so hot that your heart bakes
your writhing lover's back;
so rainy that retted streets
flow like the River Lethe,
your essence a flood of melancholy;
and the wind, the wind turns
your wheat field pages
like ancient sacred screeds
caressed by cowl sleeves.

Are you listening Heraclitus?
Change was all you left us.

Poem For David Ades

He dazzled us, this Aussie poet,
learned our seasons and taught us his.

He wrote here monuments to his grace
and graced us with the air he breathed.

Our air became his air became our air again.

We were dazzled by his words,
his smile, his eyebrows lifted,
curious, filled with wonder

at our efforts, our fragments
along the great frozen breath
of poetic time. He opened

for us a poetic season that honors
spring, warms winter, praises
summer, embraces fall. His dazzle,

now our lament, cushioned by the breeze
of his words, the swell of his oeuvre.

So long, chum. Come back soon.

Where Are You?

I wonder where you are,
a stupid question, which you
would be the first to point out.
I ask because you were always there:
I watched you solve math problems
faster than I could write the numbers
on the page. I helped you roll and
rubber-band newspapers on your route
in Cheyenne. You visited me in Denver
during Viet Nam. I tried to convince you
to declare conscientious objection, but
you objected even to that. You went up
against the government of the United States
of America, ready to face Leavenworth,
the Judge so impressed with your sincerity
that you won! You had four wives,
even more dogs—almost biblical. Still, I wonder
where you are. Sometimes I'm sure you're
the pileated woodpecker who swoops
over our yard and thrills with acrobatic
aerodynamics before gripping the peanut butter
suet with beak and tail. Maybe it's his

wingspan that makes the comparison.
On the football field at St. Mary's high
you'd stretch your arms wide and take down
the beefy corn-fed boys from other schools.
Now you fearlessly hop along our porch
even when Mugsi is there, her poodle-brain
confused by your courage.

But it's not really you.

You hadn't called your dad for two weeks
so he called the sheriff. I want you to be
this prehistoric feathered strength, this
happy hopper with a primitive call.

So where are you, Paul Visca—
ash-cover somewhere or urn-fill?
What were you thinking when it happened?
Your dad can't get into your house.
No one can find your will.

Baking Bread

In Memory of Frankie Curran

We all eat our dead, if
we loved them, that is. They die
and we carry them on our backs
like flour sacks we take home, flour

to knead into bread. Our kneading
is physical, violent. We throw
the dough onto the countertop,
and pound it with our fists, a plaint

with each punch, "Why did you
leave me here?" We mold the dough
into a metal baking casket, cover it
with a cloth shroud, and sit down

to worry it through. Will it rise?
If it does, we wrench it from its
resting place and punch and pound it
again. "How dare you abandon me

like this?" Our tears moisten the mixture
while we heat the oven and wait for a temperature
that will bake our memories and shattered hopes
in the sweltering womb-bosom oven.

The last time I saw Frankie he was Army bound.
I was a conscientious objector in Denver—1969.
I tried to dissuade him from joining the service.
We sang Christmas carols in July.

When the loaf arrives from the oven, the house
breathes the fragrance of friendship, the kind
that would lend a bed in winter, pay a lapsed heating
bill, help a pal sing Jingle Bells in summer.

On the Other Side of God's Head[5]

Phil, Frankie, Pat and Paul aren't dead,
the world is rich and gibbous,
infinity on the half-shell. The dark side
exposed, but inconsequential, not a period
but a comma, a colon, an em dash

that heralds the gleaming bulbous orb,
the harmonic hum that Heraclitus heard,
that reverberates still in the Buddhist
Om that Ginsberg chanted in Chicago
in 1968 and lives forever on YouTube.

You can believe in reincarnation
if you listen long enough to YouTube—
consciousness caught on unending sound
loops and visual, virtual eternities,
the insideoutscape on the other side
of God's cape where He She It
no longer fits and we acorns,
we sand crystals, enact universes,
admit our finitude is infinite.

November 22, 1963

Atop his chest of drawers his shower
steam enveloped my plastic turquoise case
my clock face
my snooze button he punches every school morning
tonight I wait for him
my transistors pulsing anew
tuned to 95 Fabulous KIMN in Denver
where I play his favorites   She Loves You
Please Please Me   This Boy
She Loves You is his favorite
I know by his chest heave   head wag
hands that move in drum motion without sticks
no choice when yeah yeah yeah
pounds through my tiny speakers

Tonight he forgets his towel
drips naked next to me
startled to stillness
I play   How Lovely is Thy Dwelling Place
my wires twist it out and it changes him
changes everything
I saw him standing there
tears mixing with shower water
in Brahms Requiem cleansing baptism

All his loving found its way to this music

Take Me Out of the Ballgame

Those seams loosen as I grow older,
the hardball loses its spring,
unravels slowly, becomes fusty.
In a panic I try to patch it—
look for an old friend. Quirk
was the bass player in a rock band
I drummed for in 1966.

I find him on Facebook,
that electronic sewing machine
I'm addicted to. I ask Quirk,
Does he still play guitar, has he
contacted other of our bandmates?

He answers that he has read a story of mine
on Literal Latte. Am I really an atheist?
He's concerned for my immortal soul.
He's had a personal experience of Jesus
Christ. He wants to convert me.

I've been down this road before, am shy
of lightning bolts—they leave marks,
are painful, and the smell
of burnt flesh lingers.

I write back that I'm happy
he has found a religion that
brings him peace, allows him joy and meaning,
but that, for me, religion is bullshit—
all of it. I'd appreciate it if he would
not try to convert me. I have no interest
in turning him into an atheist
and would be grateful for the same

courtesy. His answer is to unfriend me.
Ah that loving Christianity, the fierceness
of forgiveness dimly shines
across the holy sea.

I grasp that tiny ball, frazzled
seams more undone and realize
my throwing arm isn't
what it used to be.

Un Petit Mort

Maybe we shouldn't speak
of the wonders of fall.
Let us, then, notice
the russet leaves
and respect the sound
they do not make.
Let us warm hands against breath,

stand in crisp silence.
Let us listen to the whir
of wind that gyres those leaves
as they dance with orange
and amber siblings—death
gravid with color,
paraclete between summer blaze
and winter's icy peace.

Inhale the sweet odor
of earthworm and decay,
bonfires, fireplaces,
and wood stoves. Let us
prepare a place
for mortal months,
a frigid worldcorpse,
desolate mother of all.

Thanks

Doom should be ashamed of itself.
Jim Harrison

What have I missed?
When have I felt suspended,
out of it, excluded?
Oh I could dramatize
my dream of being
a professional baseball player at ten,
or my wish to be a famous
drummer in a soul band,
or the several years I thought
I desired a medical career.
These were aeries by which my
wings fluttered and failed. They

never necessitated a balaclava
to cover my disgrace, never left
me in a slurry of shame. They
were disappointments barely
noted on my personal Richter scale,
tiny taxes on the treasures that sustained
and supported my life: terrific

teachers at my undergrad colleges,
teachers who loved and cared
about me, my friends who have
blazed with me my blizzard life—
the invitation to enter the worlds
of my patients over years
of therapy practice.
My wife who made for me
a place on this earth. Our son who
knocked me off my center, showed
me the power and delight
of giving and receiving. I've lived
now ten years longer than any

man on my father's side
of the family. Ten years
longer. I bend low,
I kiss the river.

We'll All See God but Not with Our Eyes

What was Jim Harrison thinking
the day before Easter 2016,
the day he died. He lay

on his studio floor
pen in hand. He'd
been writing a poem

when his chest closed. He
believed, despite all evidence,
in the resurrection.

Was he thinking of Jesus,
His blood spoor lancing
the atmosphere as He ascended,

or was Jim preoccupied
with holding on as he fell
through the upended sky,

grasping souls of the Anasazi,
not yet inured to the mud bath
of death, or the nitwits

he'd have to put up with
in heaven? Was he thinking
of Linda, his wife of fifty years,

gone only months before,
or of the many bears he knew,
revered, and feared?

Was he scratching the chin
of a favorite birddog, maybe
his hound Rose, whom he loved

beyond expression? Maybe
he had a vision of the rear-end
of a waitress he knew in town,

how she smelled of roast
beef, potatoes, and gravy.
Was he thinking of the meadowlarks,

crows, kingfishers, and cowbirds
who accompanied him on what
he called "this bloody voyage"?

And what of the pounds
of pork roast, *foie gras*,
and quail he ate—

the gallons of vodka shooters
and Brouilly he drank,
the packs of American Spirits,

the brisket from Zingerman's,
buckets of tears shed
over impulsively opened

and consumed cans of Hormel
Chili, or the Herculean effort
expended on that famous

thirty-seven course thirteen wine lunch
he ate in France with a few cronies?
Or maybe he finally became

a bird, his lifelong ambition,
and flew into that cloud he dreamed
and shared with us.

The Theory and Practice of 43 Years

The idea is to care about her at least as much as you care about yourself.

This means asking if she wants the last piece of meatloaf before
        you put it on your plate for lunch.

This means finding something else to eat when she says
        she wants the meatloaf.

This means feeding the cats every day and cleaning the litter boxes
        because her back hurts too much to bend over.

The idea is to shift your center of gravity to the orbit of her name.

This means telling her that she can wake you up in the middle of the night
        should her pain require your touch.

It entails traveling down graveyard trails to hospitals where tape recorders
        in white coats say it's her hip, it's her back, it's her hip, it's her back.

This means playing Scrabble while the ballgame's on because
        it distracts her from the gnawing fist in her hip.

This means strapping her purse on your back so you can carry a heating
        pad in one hand and a sitting pad in another.

The idea is to celebrate the dance of dust motes on your porch, how light
        plays with shadow on a late August afternoon, the subtle fragrance

Of day lily and lilac because, at any moment, she will appear and make every
        that is absent in your world present.

Footnotes

1 The line "all nerves to serve the sun" comes from "How Soon the Servant
    Sun," in *Collected Poems*, by Dylan Thomas, New Directions, 2010.
2 In, *Collected Poems—1913-1962*, by E. E. Cummings, New York: Harcourt,
    Brace, Jovanovich, 1972
3 bleed, carnage, disrepair, depletion, flush, infrastructure, lady, Islamic,
    landscape, ripped, sad, rusted, solidarity, sprawl, stolen, stealing,
    subsidized, trillions, trapped, tombstones, unrealized, unstoppable,
    urban, wind-swept
4 Titles taken from *The Windward Shore: A Winter On The Great Lakes*, by Jerry
    Dennis
5 Title based on a line from Cesar Vallejo's poem, "I Have a Terrible
    Fear…," in Bly, Robert, *Leaping Poetry*, University of Pittsburgh Press,
    1975.

Acknowledgements

Anti-Heroin Chic: "Embrace," "Happy New Year," "Election 2016"

The Australian Rationalist: "Sartre on Smoking"

The Bear River Review: "The Unomnific Collapse of the Universe,"
　　"Hombre Y Compadre"

The Black Napkin: "Antiques," "Your Mouth"

Borfski Press: "Follow Me"

Cabildo Quarterly: "Clouds," "Measuring Time," "The Ur-Money Shot"

Chiron Review: "Farther," "Mnemosyne's Hand"
　　(nominated for a Pushcart Prize)

Climate of Opinion: Sigmund Freud in Poetry: "Identification"

Dali's Lovechild: "Floating Landscapes"

Dead King Magazine: "Chagall"

The Dunes Review: "The Old Manischewitz and the Lake"

Ekphrastic: Writing and Art on Art and Writing: "Persistence of Memory,"
　　and "En Passant."

Fifth Wednesday Journal: "On the Other Side of God's Head"

Guide To Kulcher Creative Journal: "November 22, 1963"

Hawaii Review: "Forward Pass"

KAIROS: "Casino," "Pawn Shop"

Kentucky Review: "Endurance"

November Bees: "Things That Come in Waves"

The Paterson Literary Review: "Drumbeat"

Picaroon Poetry: "Your Name in the Lake"

Pittsburgh Poetry Review: "Ode to an Avocado"

Sport Literate: "Safe at Home"

Tuck Magazine: "The March," "Office," "Bathroom Bill"

Uppagus: "The Merciful Beneficence of Repression"

VerseWrights: "Baking Bread," "Put Them All Together (With Stage
　　Directions)," "Poem for David Ades," "We'll All See God but Not
　　with Our Eyes," "Repression," "Denial"

Vox Populi: "Soulium," "Wisdom"

The Writing Disorder: "Seven Variations on a Buddha Shove," "Ten Paintings
　　by Matisse," "Ten Jazz Standards," "Rationalization,"
　　"Displacement/Sublimation"

The author wishes to thank the following for their support of this project:

Julie Albright, Jane Allen, Joan Baurer, Diane Cecily, Dar Charlebois, Richard Claraval, Jerry Dennis, Michael Dickman, Judith Dorian, Robert Fanning, Corbin and Patti Fowler, Maria Maziotti Gillan, Jodi Haven, Sandy Hooper, Lori Jareo, Chuck Kinder, Sheila Kelley, Lee Kisling, Larry Kohler, M. L. Liebler, Thomas Lynch, Ben and Nancy Manthei, William Meiners, Gary Metras, Marilu Neelis, Dagney Swan Palmer, Chuck Pfarrer, Nicholas Reading, Monica Rico, Judith Robinson, Marty Scott, Carl Sharpe, Michael Simms, Keith Taylor, Richard Tillinghast, Bob Walicki, Kevin Walzer. A special thanks to my first reader and life partner, my wife, the poet Judith Alexander Brice.

Made in the USA
Columbia, SC
14 August 2018